# SPELLING PRACTICE 2

**Word games, crosswords, similar sounds**

Richard Dawson

A Piccolo Original
Piccolo Books

# The other half

Draw in the missing half of each animal – and finish off writing their names then write the whole name underneath.

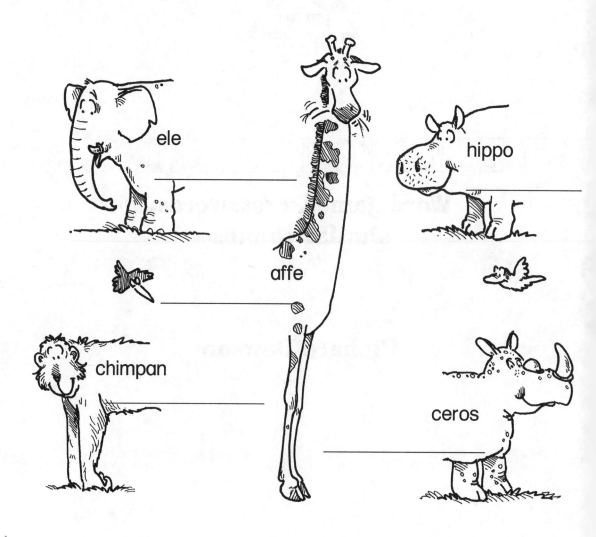

1. The animal with the long neck is the _____ .
2. The biggest of all land animals is an _____ .
3. Bananas are a favourite food of the _____ .
4. The _____ spends a lot of time in water.
5. The horn of the _____ is of great value to poachers.

# In the picture

Use the picture clues to fill in the crossword.

# Fruit and . . .

Can you write the name of each fruit on the labels?

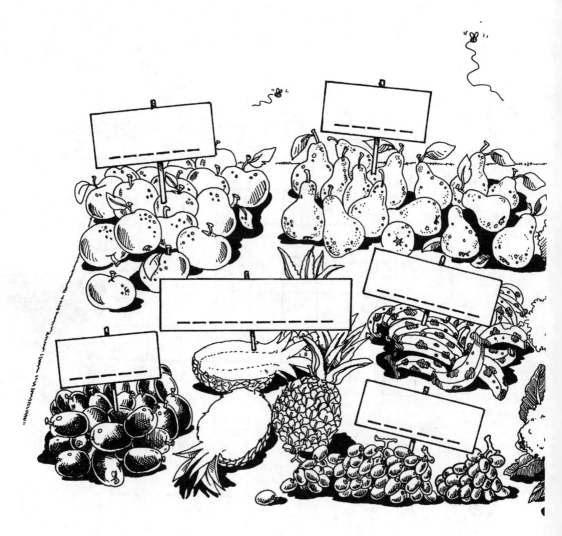

1. A partridge in a _____ tree.

2. Yellow with skins. _____

3. Eve gave one to Adam! _____

4. Make good wine. _____

5. Little Jack pulled one out! _____

6. A tropical fruit! _____

# Vegetables

Now name the vegetables.

1. A symbol for Wales! _____

2. They tempt donkeys _____

3. _____ ears!

4. Know your _____

5. Chips are made from _____

6. Large and green with yellow stripes _____

7. Green and leafy! _____

# I'm Going Crackers

Draw in the other half of the crackers to spell a word. Copy the whole word out underneath.

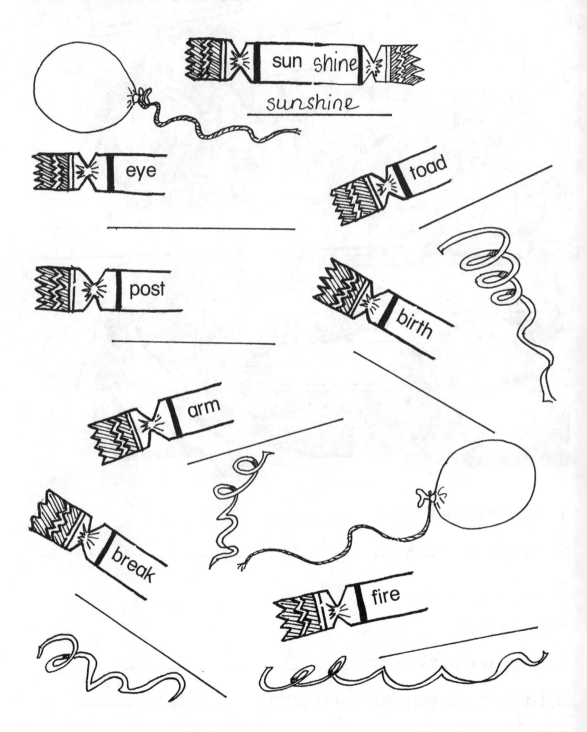

# Be the Teacher

The wrong spellings are underlined. Read the passage and cross out these spellings.

> The boys and grils rain out into the playgrownd. The rain had stoped by now but deap puddels lay on the ground. Showting and lafter filled the air as the childran splashed abowt.

Now write the passage out with the correct spellings.

_____
_____
_____
_____
_____
_____

# Months of the Year

Write out the months in order to go with each picture. Colour in the summer months.

# Tricky Words

Can you name these? Be careful – some of the words are difficult to spell.

stick out your _____    stand in a _____

ride on a _____    play in an _____

store in a _____    sing in a _____

sail in a _____    eat a _____

## Solomon Grundy's week

Write the correct phrases to go with the days of Solomon Grundy's week.

1. Born on Monday
2. _____
3. _____
4. _____

5. _____

6. _____

7. _____

Solomon Grundy, born on Monday,
Christened on Tuesday,
Married on Wednesday,
Took ill on Thursday,
Worse on Friday,
Died on Saturday,
Buried on Sunday,
This is the end of Solomon Grundy.

# Nothing to wear

Join each person to their clothes.

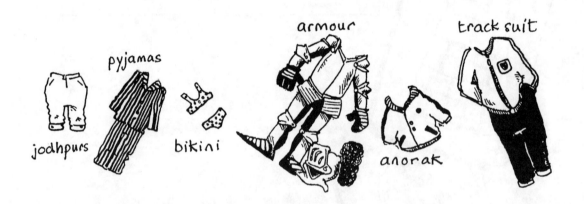

Finish these sentences

A swimmer wears a _____ .

You wear _____ in bed.

You wear an _____ when it is cold.

A sportsman wears a _____ .

A horse rider wears _____ .

A knight wears _____ .

# There or Their? Which or Witch?

In this story you have to choose between <u>which</u> or <u>witch</u> and <u>there</u> and <u>their</u>. Circle the words you think are correct. Cross out the wrong ones and then write the correct version of the story.

Which/Witch is their/there cat? Is that their/there cat over their/there? . . . or is that the which's/witch's cat? Yes, their/there cat is the ginger cat. The which's/witch's cat is the black cat over their/there. Their/there cat is over their/there.

_____
_____
_____
_____
_____
_____
_____

# Hobby dots

If you join the dots in the right order you will find out what each person is doing.

Which of these activities would you choose? Describe it and say why you like it.

_____
_____
_____
_____

# Body bits!

Can you name all the different parts of Tom's body?

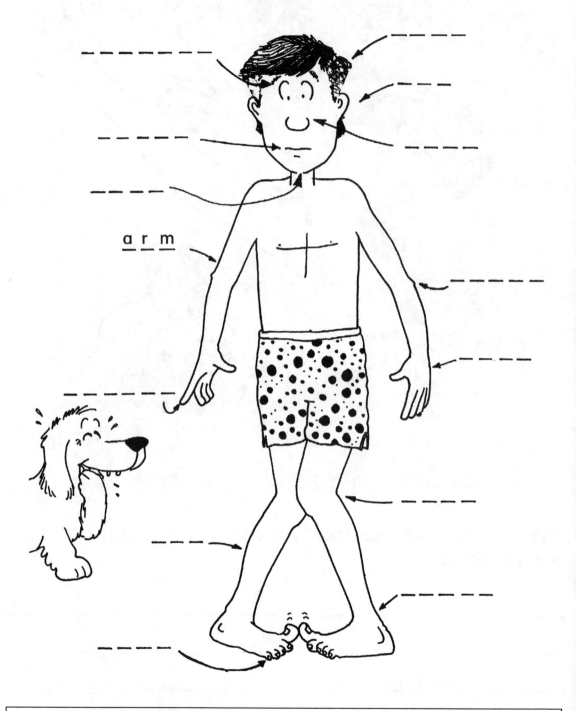

| eyebrow, mouth, chin | hair, ear, nose |
| arm, finger, leg, toes | elbow, hand, knee, ankle |

# Be the Teacher

The wrong spellings are underlined. Read the passage and cross out these spellings.

> The boys and ~~grils~~ rain out into the ~~playgrownd~~. The rain had ~~stoped~~ by now but ~~deap~~ ~~puddels~~ lay on the ground. ~~Showting~~ and ~~lafter~~ filled the air as the ~~childran~~ splashed ~~abowt~~.

Now write the passage out with the correct spellings.

_____

_____

_____

_____

_____

_____

# Be the Teacher

The wrong spellings are underlined. Read the passage and cross out these spellings.

> The boys and grils rain out into the playgrownd. The rain had stoped by now but deap puddels lay on the ground. Showting and lafter filled the air as the childran splashed abowt.

Now write the passage out with the correct spellings.

_____

_____

_____

_____

_____

_____

# Be the Teacher

The wrong spellings are underlined. Read the passage and cross out these spellings.

> The boys and grils rain out into the playgrownd. The rain had stoped by now but deap puddels lay on the ground. Showting and lafter filled the air as the childran splashed about.

Now write the passage out with the correct spellings.

# It's One . . . . . or the Other

Both words sound the same, but which is the correct one to use? Write it out to complete the sentence.

1. son, sun
   The _____ was so hot we had to eat our picnic in the shade of a tree.

2. hair, hare      stile, style
   After his visit to the barber, Winston was very pleased with his new _____ _____.

3. seam, seem
   Dad decided he must go on a diet after he had split the _____ in his trousers.

4. bales, bails
   With an excellent throw, Rajesh knocked the _____ from the incoming batsman's wicket.

5. plain, plane
   His _____ out of control the pilot was forced to eject and parachute to safety.

6. idol, idle
   _____ Jack lazed around all day long.

7. fair, fare
   The bus _____ to the _____ ground cost 15p.

8. guerilla, gorilla
   The _____ looked very sad in his cage at the zoo.

9. place, plaice
   '_____ and chips three times please.'

10. doe, dough
    The baker forgot to put the yeast into his _____ and the bread was a real flop!

# Map work

Colour all the countries green that are spelt correctly, and discover Europe!

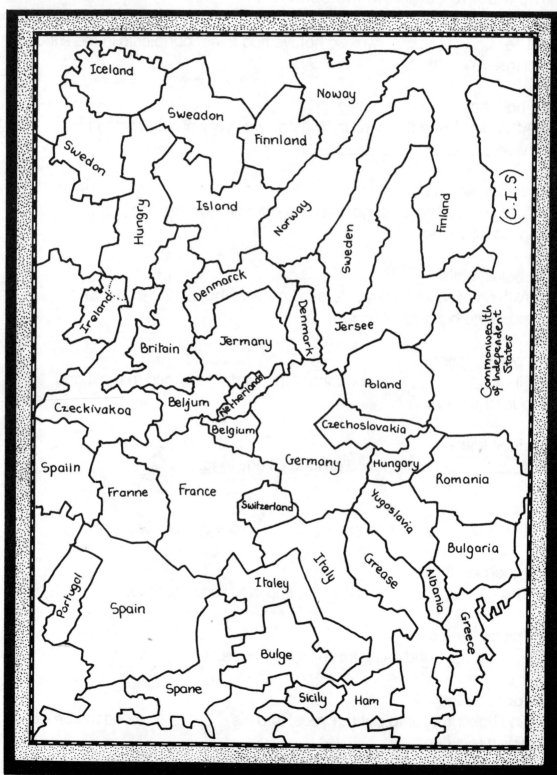

# I before E

The old, rule is 'i before e except after c' or when ei says a as in eight. Fill in the correct letters so that the words are properly spelt. Join each worm to its frog.

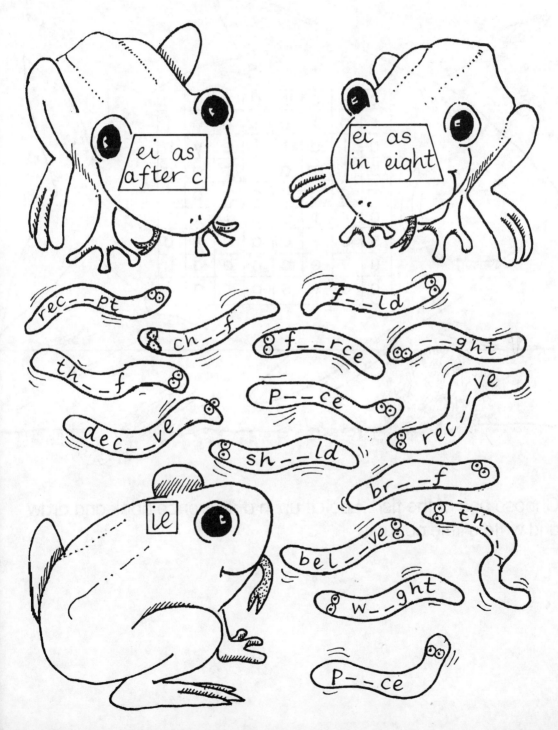

# Something Fishy

What has the fat shark eaten? Can you find the hidden fish? There are 10.

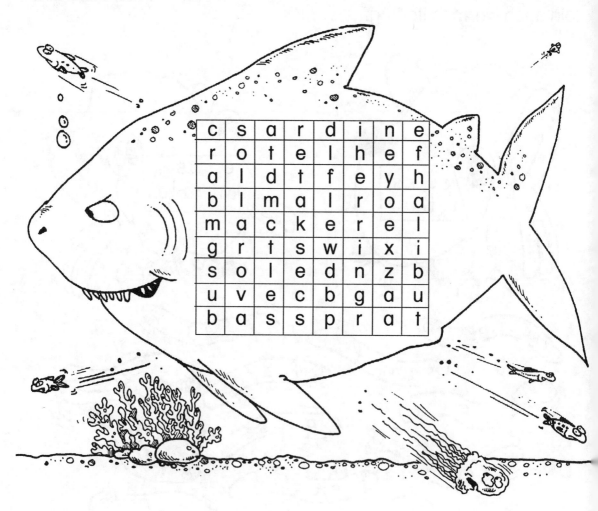

| c | s | a | r | d | i | n | e |
| r | o | t | e | l | h | e | f |
| a | l | d | t | f | e | y | h |
| b | l | m | a | l | r | o | a |
| m | a | c | k | e | r | e | l |
| g | r | t | s | w | i | x | i |
| s | o | l | e | d | n | z | b |
| u | v | e | c | b | g | a | u |
| b | a | s | s | p | r | a | t |

Choose one of the fish. Look it up in a reference book and draw and write a little about it.

# On Tow

Find the word and fill in the caravan. Write the whole word below.

a ship's load

___

a garden vegetable

___

floor covering

___

a Christmas hymn

___

a cardboard case

___

deep red

___

to cut into slices

___

a house on wheels

___

# Tion or Sion?

Finish off the whole word each time. Use a dictionary to look up the meanings and write them in your own words.

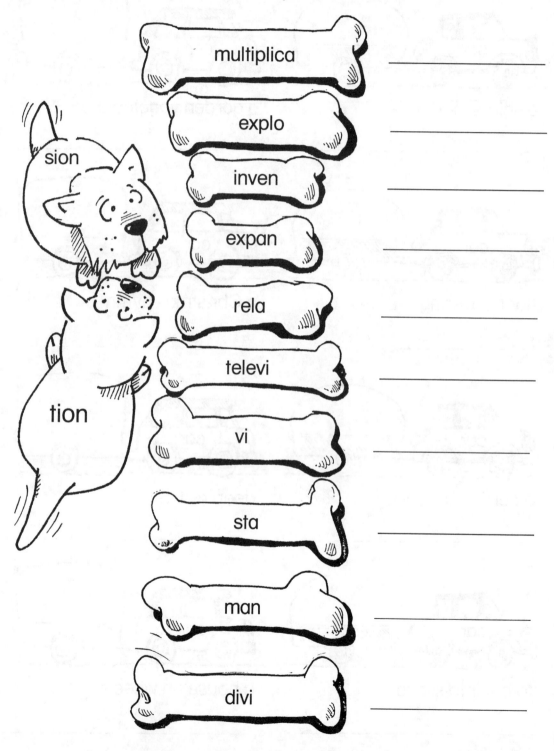

multiplica

explo

inven

expan

rela

televi

vi

sta

man

divi

# Window Shopping

Write in the names of the shops. Look carefully at what each shop sells.

Now answer these questions

1. Where could you buy glasses? _____

2. Who sells fish? _____

3. Where could you buy garlic sausage? _____

4. A new house? Then visit the _____.

5. Baked beans, soap powder, cereal can be bought at the _____.

6. Old and valuble things can be bought in the _____.

# On the Farm

Can you find the farm machinery? If you join the dots in the right order the vehicles will appear!

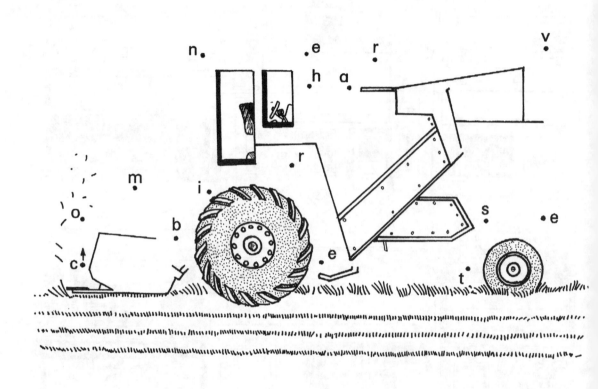

# Happy Families

Write out the names for male, female and young for each animal family.

\_ \_ \_ \_          \_ \_ \_          \_ \_ \_ \_ \_

A number of pigs is called a _____

\_ \_ \_          \_ \_ \_          \_ \_ \_ \_

A number of sheep is called a _____

\_ \_ \_ \_          \_ \_ \_          \_ \_ \_ \_

A number of cattle is called a _____

A number of dogs is called a _____

# Weather Watchers

Here is the weather forecast.
Can you write in the missing words?

What is the weather like in the North? _____

Where is the sun shining? _____

On the S.E coast it is _____

Where is it raining? _____

It is snowing in the _____

# Family Photos

Can you work out who's who from each picture?

Can you fill in the gaps?

<u>b r o t h e r</u>

Draw your family tree here

**Answer the sums. . . . . . in words!**

three times three equals _____

ten plus seven equals _____

eleven minus six equals _____

fifteen divided by three equals _____

nine times nine equals _____

seven multiplied by eight equals _____

nine add eleven equals _____

# Sssh . . . !

Find the hidden words. The clues at the bottom of the page will help you find them. Circle your answers.

1. A snail has one on his back
2. We wear them on our feet
3. It sails on the sea
4. Where do you buy things from?
5. Knives, scissors, pins and needles are
6. A vicious fish
7. Squares triangles etc
8. Out of the sun
9. Bright
10. To push
11. Another name for money
12. A fairy might give you this
13. It swims in a bowl
14. To turn red
15. To hurry
16. Be quiet!
17. A small tree
18. To squash
19. Opposite to pull
20. Snow turns into this

Fill in the crossword, there is an answer from each page!

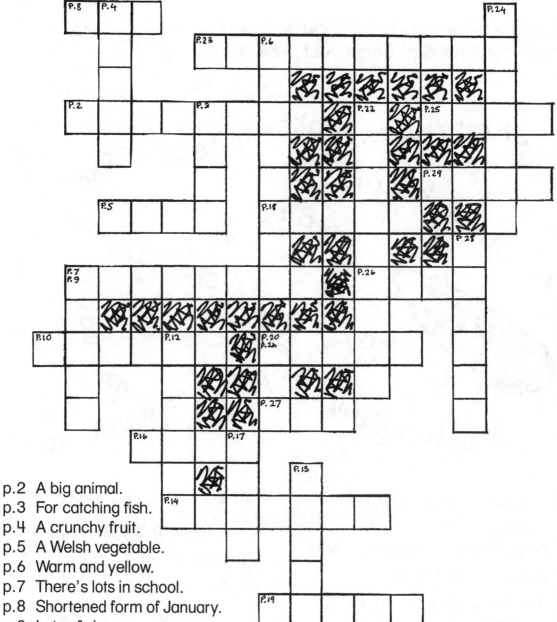

p.2 A big animal.
p.3 For catching fish.
p.4 A crunchy fruit.
p.5 A Welsh vegetable.
p.6 Warm and yellow.
p.7 There's lots in school.
p.8 Shortened form of January.
p.9 Lots of singers.
p.10 The first working day.
p.12 Metal clothes.
p.13 She flies on a broomstick.
p.14 You need a book for this.
p.16 There's ten on your feet.
p.17 Where two pieces of cloth join.
p.18 This country is like a long leg.
p.19 The head of a tribe.
p.20 .... and chips.
p.21 Sing it at Christmas.
p.22 Dynamite makes one.
p.23 He sells fish.
p.24 A farmer drives this.
p.25 A number of dogs.
p.26 Cold flakes.
p.27 Shortened version of father.
p.28 A score!
p.29 You buy from here.

30

# Answers

**p.2**
elephant
hippopotamus
giraffe
chimpanzee
rhinoceros
1. giraffe
2. elephant
3. chimpanzee
4. hippopotamus
5. rhinoceros

**p.3**
1. goose
2. swimming pool
3. hook
4. broom
5. moon
6. look
7. spoon
8. cook
9. rook

**p.4**
1. pear
2. banana
3. apple
4. grapes
5. plum
6. pineapple

**p.5**
1. leek
2. carrots
3. cauliflower
4. onions
5. potatoes
6. marrow
7. cabbage

**p.6**
sunshine
eyelid
postman
armchair
breakfast
fireman
toadstool
birthday

**p.7**
girls
ran
playground
stopped
deep
puddles
shouting
laughter
children
about

**p.8**
January
February
March
April
May
June
July
August
September
October
November
December

**p.9**
choir
tongue
biscuit
queue
yacht
bicycle
orchestra
cupboard

**p.10**
Monday
Tuesday
Wednesday
Thursday
Friday
Saturday
Sunday

**p.12**
1. bikini
2. pyjamas
3. anorak
4. tracksuit
5. jodhpurs
6. armour

**p.13**
which
their
their
there
witch's
their
witch's
there
Their
there

**p.14**
skipping
tennis
hockey
skateboarding

**p.15**
football
skiing
reading
chess

**p.16**
eyebrow
mouth
chin
hand
legs
toes
hair
ear
nose
arm
elbow
finger
knee
ankle

**p.17**
1. sun
2. hair style
3. seam
4. bails
5. plane
6. idle
7. fare fair
8. gorilla
9. plaice
10. dough

**p.18**
Iceland
Norway
Sweden
Finland
Britain
Ireland
Denmark
Netherlands
Poland
Hungary
Czechoslovakia
Romania
Yugoslavia
Bulgaria
Switzerland
France
Portugal
Spain
Italy
Albania
Greece
Sicily

**p.19**
receipt
chief
field
thief
fierce
eight
piece
receive
deceive
shield
brief
believe
their
weight
piece

**p.20**
sardine
cod
skate
herring
halibut
sprat
bass
crab
mackerel
sole

**p.21**
cargo
carrot
carpet
carol
carton
carmine
carve
caravan

**p.22**
multiplication
explosion
invention
expansion
relation
television
vision
station
mansion
division

**p.23**
1. optician
2. fishmonger
3. delicatessen
4. estate agent
5. grocer
6. antique

**p.24**
combine harvester
tractor
trailer

**p.25**
boar   sow   piglet
herd
ram   ewe   lamb
flock
bull   cow   calf
herd
dog   bitch   puppy
pack

**p.26**
cloudy
rain
sunshine
thunder and lightning
frost
snow
wind

**p.27**
brother
mother
grandparents
baby
father
sister
aunt
uncle

**p.28**
nine
seventeen
five
five
eighty one
fifty six
twenty

**p.29**
1. shell
2. shoes
3. ship
4. shops
5. sharp
6. shark
7. shapes
8. shade
9. shine
10. shove
11. cash
12. wish
13. fish
14. blush
15. rush
16. hush
17. bush
18. crush
19. push
20. slush